SOCCER LEGENDS ALPHABET

WOMEN

Words by Robin Feiner

Aa

A is for Michelle Akers. Whether as a goal-scoring forward or as a defensive midfielder, Akers did whatever it took to win. She won the Golden Boot at the inaugural Women's World Cup, was named FIFA Female Player of the Century and was one of only two women named in the FIFA 100. Truly an all-time great!

B is for **B**irgit Prinz. This three-time FIFA World Player of the Year and prolific goal scorer led Germany to back-to-back World Cup triumphs. She also won three UEFA Champions League titles with FFC Frankfurt! Prinz now serves as the German national team's sports psychologist.

C is for **C**hristine Sinclair. 'Sincy' has led the Canadian front line for nearly two decades and become one of the highest scoring players in international soccer history. Canadian fans will never forget her heroic hat-trick in a contentious defeat to the USA at the 2012 Olympics.

D is for **D**iana Matheson. A diminutive midfield dynamo, standing just 5'0" tall, 'D' is the engine that drives Team Canada. Her stoppage-time winner in the 2012 Olympics bronze medal game won Canada its first-ever medal in women's soccer.

E is for **E**lisabetta Vignotto. In the days before the official Women's World Cup, there were few teams better than Italy – and no player better than Vignotto, who led the Azzure to multiple 'Mundialito' titles in the 1980s. 'Betty' retired with 107 international goals, the world record until it was broken by Mia Hamm.

F is for Formiga.
Born Miraildes Maciel Mota, she was given the nickname Formiga – meaning 'ant' – for her hard-working and unselfish style of play. A constant in the Brazilian midfield, Formiga has appeared in a record seven World Cups and seven Olympic tournaments. Truly the ultimate team player!

G is for Carin Jennings-Gabarra. One of the greatest dribblers the game has ever seen, her teammates called her 'Crazy Legs' and 'Gumby' for her ability to bend and twist. As part of the 'Triple-Edged Sword' with Akers and Heinrichs, Gabarra dominated the first Women's World Cup and was honored with the Golden Ball.

H is for Mia **H**amm.
A true sports icon, Hamm was the most recognizable player in women's soccer during its rise in the 1990s. Scoring goals and winning games at every level, she ended her career as the highest scorer in international soccer history and was named to the FIFA 100 list by Pelé.

**I is for Hege Riise.
This Norwegian midfield maestra was known as "the woman with six pairs of eyes" for her creativity and ability to see plays before they happened. She is one of just three women to win a World Cup, European Championship and Olympic gold medal.**

J is Julie Foudy.
After serving as either captain or co-captain of the U.S. National Team for 14 years, 'Loudy Foudy' founded the Julie Foudy Sports Leadership Academy, which encourages young girls to excel on and off the pitch.

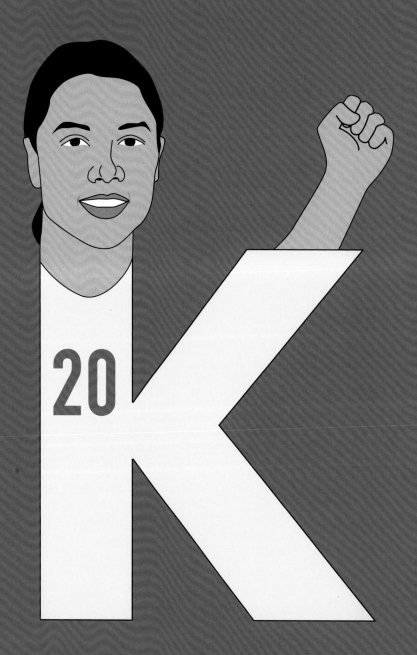

K is for Sam **K**err.
This Chelsea forward, and Matildas captain, has shattered records for both club and country. Hailing from Australia, she is the all-time leading scorer in the NWSL, and the only female player to have won the Golden Boot in three different leagues and continents.

L is for Carli **L**loyd.
In the biggest game of her life, the 2015 World Cup Final, Lloyd played the best game of her life. She scored a hat-trick in under 16 minutes, the third goal coming on an audacious chip from the midfield line. No wonder she's a two-time FIFA Player of the Year!

M is for Alex **M**organ.
The current face of U.S. soccer, Morgan is a star on and off the field. A goal-scoring machine, she used speed and finesse to torment defenses and drive the USA to back-to-back World Cup titles. She's also authored a series of books for middle school readers and starred in the movie, 'Alex & Me.'

N is for **N**adine Angerer. Beginning her career as a striker, Angerer went on to become one of the greatest goalkeepers of all time after filling in for an injured teammate. She cemented her legacy at the 2007 World Cup, where she didn't concede a goal the entire tournament and stopped a penalty from Marta in the final.

**O is for Carla Overbeck.
A reliable central defender,
Carla teamed with Joy
Fawcett to form the heart
of a resolute U.S. defense
throughout the 1990s. Serving
as captain for eight years,
she played every minute of
the 1995 and 1999 World
Cups, and the 1996 Olympics.**

P is for Lily **P**arr.
A trailblazer on and off the pitch, Parr dominated the women's game in England during a remarkable career stretching from 1919 to 1951. Standing 5'10" and possessing "a kick like a mule," Parr used her tremendous skill and power to score more than 900 goals. A legend among legends!

Q is for Sun **Q**ingmei. Despite the disapproval of her parents, who wouldn't let her out to play soccer, Sun grew up to become a mainstay on the Chinese national team through the 1980s and 90s. She proudly won a silver medal at the 1996 Olympics.

R is for Megan **R**apinoe. Known for playing skillfully on the field and fighting for justice off it, Rapinoe is a fearless player and person. The lavender-haired winger took center stage at the 2019 World Cup, scoring clutch goals and celebrating in style when she won the Golden Ball for best player.

S is for Homare Sawa. Playing 23 years with the Japanese national team, Sawa experienced many legendary moments. Captaining Japan to World Cup glory in 2011 and scoring the dramatic equalizer in the final was one of her finest. She was awarded the Golden Ball, Golden Boot and the FIFA Player of the Year Award that year.

T is for **T**iffeny Milbrett. Though she also excelled at basketball and track and field, 'Tiff' always dreamed of being a soccer player: "It was really, really my goal, in my heart and in my blood." She scored an even 100 goals in her U.S. national team career, including the winning goal in the 1996 Olympic gold medal game. Dream accomplished!

U is for Sun Wen.
The star of China's golden generation, Wen was a gifted playmaker and scorer who was deadly with either foot. This 1999 Golden Ball and Golden Boot winner gave everything she could for the Steel Roses, and was named FIFA Women's Player of the Century. A well-deserved honor for such a legendary player!

V is for Marta Vieira da Silva. A five-time World Player of the Year, with a record 17 World Cup goals, Marta is the greatest of all time. She is magical with the ball at her feet, regularly scoring goals that others can only dream of. At the 2019 World Cup, she delivered an impassioned message to Brazilian girls: "Cry in the beginning so you can smile in the end."

W is for Abby **W**ambach. This powerful forward knows how to use her head – literally! Seventy-seven of her all-time record 184 international goals have come off headers, none more famous than her 122nd-minute equalizer against Brazil in the 2011 World Cup quarters.

X is for Shannon Bo**x**x.
In spite of illness, she fought her way to the highest levels of women's soccer. After personal disappointments in back-to-back World Cups – receiving a card and missing a penalty kick in elimination games – Boxx was a member of USA's 2015 championship team. Never give up!

Yy

Y is for **Y**ūki Nagasato. Always striving to be the best, Nagasato left her comfort zone in Japan to play professionally in Germany, England, the USA and Australia. A trophy case that includes a World Cup and a UEFA Champions League title shows that she made the right decision.

Z is for **Z**hao Lihong.
'The Cat' was a fixture on China's left side in the 1990s, regularly beating defenders off the dribble and sending dangerous crosses into the box. She was a member of China's 1996 silver medal team and was named an all-star at the 1999 World Cup.

The ever-expanding legendary library

EXPLORE THESE LEGENDARY ALPHABETS & MORE AT WWW.ALPHABETLEGENDS.COM

SOCCER LEGENDS ALPHABET - WOMEN
www.alphabetlegends.com

Published by Alphabet Legends Pty Ltd in 2023
Created by Beck Feiner
Copyright © Alphabet Legends Pty Ltd 2023

9780648672401